Charlotte Moss
ENTERTAINS

Charlotte Moss
ENTERTAINS

RIZZOLI
NEW YORK

New York · Paris · London · Milan

Contents

Introduction

Have you ever considered how much ridiculous pomposity surrounds the word entertaining? . . . I wish there was a word to replace that rather stilted one. I like better, "having your friends to the house." — DOROTHY DRAPER

How often do you think about where you came from, the place where you were born and grew up? If you still live in your hometown, well, I guess the answer is obvious. If at some point you moved away and settled elsewhere, you probably have gentle reminders of all sorts. We have friends, fond memories, and favorite gathering places, the local park where families gathered for boat rides and baseball on weekends, the public library and the place you always liked to sit and read, or the neighborhood market where the check-out girl always slipped you something sweet. We carry these moments with us wherever we go.

Then, there are some of us who, after moving away, realize that we took something else with us. We took something that could not be packed, crated, or shipped. We took a lot more than the luggage, the furniture, treasured objects, the convertible, grandfather's canoe, and our mother's linens. What we took was a bond. In my case, it was a bond to all things Southern. Like signing a pact, it is a connection that can never be severed because it runs too damn deep. Like Spanish moss clinging to cypress trees in a swamp, my Southern roots will stay with me, and follow me everywhere.

Southern women look after each other; are fiercely loyal; and, let's put it on the table, are credited with inventing hospitality. At the same time they can be embarrassingly irreverent while redeeming themselves with a wicked sense of humor that can make you laugh until the mascara runs. No one else in the country has shared as many recipes as the Junior League through their cookbooks of the South. Family recipes are available in these nothing-fancy, spiral-bound cookbooks that have been produced in the hundreds of thousands, and reprinted countless times. There's not an author I know who wouldn't die for those stats. I think those numbers speak to the authenticity that bubbles to the surface of every family recipe in those books. Southerners share and have been for generations. No Babe Paley, Gloria Guinness shenanigans here.

Our recipe books ooze with stained notes handed down from mothers, grandmothers, and girlfriends. They are tried, true, and beyond just tempting; they have been served repeatedly, because that is what we were taught to do—cook, serve, please. A Southern hostess will be up all night fussing, puttering, fluffing the house

because company's coming tomorrow, and everything must be just so. I witnessed these activities firsthand many times, watching my mother "fuss."

Every year I have two big gatherings of girls at home: my annual Christmas buffet and my summer Caftan Caucus. I love planning every detail, including the Southern buffet, and look forward to seeing every person and, of course, hearing a symphony of Southern accents amidst the New Yorkers. I confess to going into a post-gathering funk when everyone scatters and departs. It's just too darn quiet.

Delightedly I learned that outside the South the Southern connection was enough to get one invited to a party with other ham biscuit– and pimento cheese–craving expats. Everyone you met knew someone else you knew, and on it went. Laughing and storytelling went on into the night. I remember everyone helping out, cleaning up, and never missing a beat. With a casserole dish in one hand, cocktail in the other, and talking fast to get to the punch line. A good storytelling Southerner knows you've got to hold your ground—keeping your audience rapt or else you would lose your place and the next tall tale was at the ready.

We are fortunate to have such diversity in our own country, and when I look at the South I feel even more blessed to have been raised in a place with such rich historical, cultural, artistic, culinary, and literary traditions. Where else in the country does one discuss Low Country and Creole food

and understand how different they are and from what part of the South they call home?

That heritage is a lot to ponder. In fact, I feel a sense of responsibility to carry it, and all that it represents, with me everywhere.

I have parked myself in front of my iPad to write this book so many times. Countless fruitless attempts later I decided *not* to write it at all. Months of agony proved my initial reactions spot on. Now, hold on to that thought for a moment; we'll come back to it.

So many thoughtful texts have been written in the past about food, cooking, and entertaining—words presented with joy, humor, passion, and volumes of experience. To me the task seemed daunting, to write something that had not already been written.

My approach has always been to share my own experiences and to bring history forward—combined with a dose of history by engaging the influencers of the past, which has been a theme in my life and in my writing.

When I was initially considering the theme of this book, I realized that I have a problem with the word *entertaining*. It reminds me of what a comedian does, what going to the movies or a great Broadway show is all about. The word can also evoke images of state dinner formality, the frightening thought of the boss and his wife coming to dinner, and your mother-in-law's scrutinizing, hypercritical eye. Furthermore, it conjures up thoughts and images of hours of preparation and labor. It sounds so serious. It suggests long-range planning, phone calls, emails, and reminder notes. Planning menus; testing recipes;

organizing clever place settings, centerpieces, and calligraphed place cards and menu cards. Ironing table linens, polishing silver, holding each glass up to the light to make sure it is clear and sparkling. And those decorating projects that you've been dithering about and dragging your heels on—it's now or never.

Oh, yes, and who's doing the cooking, the serving, and all the cleanup?

Let's face it, entertaining *is* work, but it is not supposed to be a chore. The care and feeding of friends and family is one of life's great pleasures. Introducing people, the buzz of laughter and conversation, the smile acknowledging that something tastes great, being told everything looks beautiful, clean plates! The exhilaration of a successful evening, well, what could possibly be more gratifying? Once you've done it enough times, and with confidence, you will then graduate to what all great hosts and hostesses are able to do—spontaneous entertaining. Over time, one learns how to stock the pantry and the bar. And one aquires the elegant shortcuts, including using your everyday silver so no emergency polishing is required. One can quickly assemble pressed linens, a favorite playlist, and a bouquet picked up at a local shop.

You've read it all before, I'm sure, in the books your mother gave you: ones by Emily Post, Amy Vanderbilt, and Martha Stewart. All the etiquette and entertaining mavens have laid out the protocol, the party-planning tips, guides on etiquette, how to expand a dinner to eight from six because your husband called and said, "Oh, by the way, one of the guys in our San Francisco office brought his wife to town." How to be a good hostess: making introductions, keeping conversations going, knowing when to divert the topic of a conversation, and being aware of every last detail that goes into the planning of a good party.

A good hostess always has a sense of humor and knows how to finesse it when the soufflé falls: "Oh, it's a special pudding recipe one of my English friends gave me, light as a feather." I clearly remember my first dinner disaster, the night my husband invited his boss from California to dinner for the first time. Sparing you lots of the details, my hollandaise separated. I had made it so many times before, how could this happen tonight? I was mortified, but no one knew. Quickly I grabbed some vinaigrette, drizzled it on the asparagus, topped it off with some chopped parsley, and no one knew the difference. Years later when I knew the boss better, I told him the story and we all had a good laugh.

The most terrifying moment in my entertaining history was when I was hosting a cocktail party for the Irish Georgian Society, with Sybil Connolly and Desmond Guinness as guests of honor. When the caterer arrived, I asked where the champagne was? To which he responded, "We thought you were supplying it!" My heart sank. Thank goodness for a nimble caterer with lots of connections; he called in a few favors and sent his truck to collect champagne from

TABLE SETTINGS

Charlotte

Marlen

several of his restaurateur friends. Finally in the pantry, chilled and corks being popped, no one was ever the wiser.

As I said at the outset, there are too many good books available that contain all the whats, ifs, how-tos and definitely the nots. But, I thought I might give you some thoughts that have guided me over the years. Nothing complicated, no rules, no finger wagging—just ideas. Once you finish reading them, you will say to yourself, "So, what's new?" To which I will respond, "Absolutely nothing, except my experiences, to which you will add your own over time."

THE KEY IS YOU. Put every bit of yourself in the details, and they will be noticed and appreciated. It is your party. You may have others help you execute it, but the decisions are yours.

KNOW YOUR STRENGTHS. Do what you are good at, and, if you can, hire other people to do the rest.

SENDING THE INVITATION. So much has been written on this subject. When I first started entertaining in the pre-digital age, I sent out engraved invitations. We move much faster now and communicate at the same warp speed. So this is my take on the subject: if you have the benefit of time, mail an invitation. If you are not inclined to paper, then make phone calls and follow up with reminder notes, paper or digital. Another way is PaperlessPost.com. You can create your own invitation graphics, colors,

fonts, even the lining of the faux envelope. Your guests respond to Paperless Post, and you can view the list, along with their comments. In summary, select your own method. All are acceptable today for informal occasions; formal dinners and events require printed invitations.

RELAX. The key to giving your guests the signal that you are having a good time is to relax and savor the company and the atmosphere. If you are stressed, everyone will notice and they too will respond similarly.

NO CHEATING. Two things you cannot cheat on: food and flowers. I might also add wine, if it is to be included. Rule of thumb, buy the best you can afford. Do your homework and make friends with a salesperson at your local wine shop—you can get great tips and have a friend for life. Give the wines a taste—your guests should not be the ones test-driving your selections. Put the label in a book with your comments. The same goes for the menu: never attempt a new recipe with guests; always try it yourself first.

HELP! If you need to hire waiters, make sure you have enough and take time to familiarize them with your home so they can function without bothering you. Because I often give large dinners we have been blessed with a number of gentlemen who have worked for us for years. Their ability to navigate the house and know where things are stored is one of the keys to a successful party. Not to mention the fact that it makes me completely relaxed and ready to receive my guests breathing easily.

DON'T FORGET THE TUNES. There is nothing like music to set the tone for a party. You must have music, and it should reflect and reinforce the mood of the evening. Music at cocktail time is key; it relaxes people and simply puts them in a good mood. Remember, at dinner, it is all about the conversation; therefore there should be no music. Playlists are easy to create and by doing so you have further personalized your evening.

SHOP YOUR CLOSET. Centerpieces for the table do not always have to be flowers. Study your cupboards and closets for items to use. Use what you have; you will surprise yourself and gain confidence at the same time. Look around on tabletops and in bookcases; I am sure you will rediscover something you have forgotten about that can create a story on your table at your next dinner.

CREATE A WARDROBE FOR YOUR TABLE. I have been collecting plates and linens for a long time. Part of the fun is creating table schemes for lunches or dinners. After all, I am a decorator. I can't help myself. It gives me great pleasure. A table setting is like a collage: you start with an idea, one item, then build around it, layering in everything needed to complete the story. You'll surprise yourself as you begin to layer with items

you own. Not only is it a great decorating exercise, it's a great opportunity to take inventory and assess your needs.

MIX IT UP . . . and I don't just mean the cocktails. Experiment with different combinations of china patterns. A set of decorated salad plates from your grandmother can liven up a white dinner service. The blue-and-white china that you've been collecting for years: go ahead, use ten different dinner plates; don't wait until you have a complete set of one thing. When you are happy with your new setting, photograph it and keep an album on your phone or elsewhere; it will be easier the next time because you have a record.

USE YOUR LINENS. Crisp and clean—and beautifully ironed—are always the watchwords for table linens. If you need to have one set of napkins, hands down I would suggest the best quality white napkins you can afford. I'd even suggest 24-inch napkins, called "lapkins" because they are perfect for buffets as well as seated dinners.

LIGHT THE CANDLES, PLEASE. To me nothing is more mood enhancing and downright sexy than candlelight. In the front hall, in the living room, and at the table the gentle flickering of light sets the mood. Kill the overheads and dim the lamps—let the party begin.

PLEASE BE SEATED. Place-card seating requires a hostess to consider her guests and who will be compatible with whom. There are protocols for more formal dinners that any book of etiquette will spell out for you. Do not make your guests guess where to sit, or have to choose themselves. Thoughtful placement prevents awkward moments and shows that you, the hostess, have done all the thinking to ensure a relaxed and successful evening.

NOT FOR DINING ROOMS ONLY. The dining table, of course, is the natural location for a dinner. Buffet dinners can have guests seating themselves in your living room or family room or wherever. Do you have a fireplace in the family room or library? What about a cozy dinner for four on the screened porch? You know your home, what other spots will work for you?

MAKE A TOAST. It is always a nice way to kick off the evening. Humor and brevity are always appreciated, and planning what to say is key.

DRESSING FOR DINNER. Every host/hostess should allow enough time to get ready for their own party, with a little buffer time for just relaxing and checking everything one last time.

PRACTICE, PRACTICE. I know it may seem redundant to say it again, but practice is the key. As with anything that requires a bit of proficiency, being a host/hostess is no exception. The more practice you have, the more confidence you'll gain, and I guarantee, the more you will be sending invitations to future parties.

SETTING THE TABLE IS EVERYDAY DECORATING. This is where you begin with practice. Setting a table is something we can do everyday, not just when entertaining. In addition to being a confidence builder, it is simply a civilized thing to do. Hospitality begins at home, and setting the table with care and flair for yourself and your family is where it all begins. Once you've got that down, then the parties can begin.

SURPRISE, SURPRISE. I think a good way to make any event memorable is to add an element of surprise, or something that puts your stamp on it. This can include a special cocktail you have made for the evening, your table design, an entertainment, a soufflé for dessert, or a small gift as a parting gesture. Whatever it is, it should spell fun; after all, that is why you got everyone together, right?

FOR THE RECORD. I believe in keeping a record of all of my parties, and I do it for two very specific reasons. One, I want to enjoy the memory in the future. Two, and most practical, I want to remember who was at a dinner so that the next time I can mix up the guest list. Same with the menu, I would not want to serve the same food, or set the table the same way. It is not a complicated thing to do; it just takes a little time. I view that time as a great investment, where the payback is future successful entertaining and happy guests.

SETTING
THE TABLE *IS*
EVERYDAY
DECORATING

Name something that you do three times a day that gives you an opportunity to practice and to keep getting better at it. Unless you are a professional athlete, a ballerina, or a rock star, there aren't that many things that we do daily, and multiple times per day, that give us a chance to improve our skills. But eat we do, and setting the table is our chance to make mealtime with family a special time. Even if you are setting the table once—for family dinner, for yourself and your partner—you can express yourself and create a setting conducive not only to enjoying a meal but also to encouraging relaxation and an environment for conversation about the day. There were five children at the table when I was growing up. When the table was set (and we all contributed to the pre-meal chores), we knew it was time to come together for the evening. There was no use debating *if* the television (in the days before iPads and mobile telephones) was to be turned off, and of course, none of us hesitated putting the homework on hold. We also knew that dinnertime was the time to recount our day's activities—updates on an algebra test, an oral report in English, a football scrimmage, and cheerleading practice. Everyone talked about something, and everyone else listened, sitting up straight, with napkin in lap and elbows where they ought to be. Knowing how to fold a napkin and where each utensil was placed—once learned and practiced, and heaven knows we had enough of that—were a source of pride and satisfaction. What I learned then has been with me ever since. Little did I know that I would be writing a book about it years later. I read and hear about families never eating at the table together, about devices being permitted on the table, about how conversation is minimal, and even how utensils are used sparingly. Judging by what you witness in restaurants today, it is obvious that no one has shown some people, and I mean adults not just children, that the chin does not have to kiss the plate, the instrument is called a

fork (not a pitchfork), and a knife is for cutting, not sawing. Good heavens. Thanks for listening.

As a designer and someone who believes that we should make every effort to make our surroundings as beautiful as possible, I find that with minimal effort we can bring beauty to the dinner table. It does not matter what you decide to use in setting your table; the key is to make the time and do it neatly and thoughtfully. Time spent at the table should be pleasant, making us look forward to the next meal and the chance to spend time together. The dining table is the single piece of furniture in the house where we gather together not just for nourishment but also for conversation and companionship, a place where we gather to celebrate special occasions and to continue family traditions.

The more you experiment with what you have in setting the table, the more confidence you will gain and the more fun you will have. You will find yourself unwittingly eyeballing placemats and napkins, and picking up a vase here, a basket there, to decorate the center of the table. Creating table schemes or stories for the table is not very different from the decorating that I do every day; however, once a decorating plan is implemented and installed it is there to stay for a while. That is why I encourage everyone to embrace setting the table as everyday decorating. It is a chance to hone your skills, develop your own personal style, and practice for your parties of the future.

Mealtime will be a joyous time, as it should be. A meal carefully prepared, or a takeout meal, can be presented in the same way; no one will be the wiser. The point is just to do it.

Why not make every day an occasion?

Dining in the Garden

There's no place I would rather sit down to a meal than on our terrace in East Hampton. To be outside every moment is the goal after arriving from the city. To have coffee outdoors in the morning is no big deal to some people, but when you live in New York City, a soft breeze and the sound of birds are a salve for the soul. The table on the terrace is always set for lunch. Tablecloths are de rigueur, because they act as backgrounds for new combinations of china, glassware, and flatware. And always, there are flowers—blooms from the garden, topiaries, geraniums, or a potted annual. It's casual dining, and it is a pleasure to decorate the table to make our meals together colorful, fun, and always changing.

"*Everything tastes better outdoors.*"
— CLAUDIA RODEN

Buffets

I love a buffet—guests can select exactly what they want.

A buffet dinner is one of my favorite ways to entertain a group larger than my dining room table can accommodate. In fact, one of the great benefits of a buffet is that it leaves you room to be a bit more elastic with the size of your guest list, and free to add at the last minute. Count your chairs, stools, ottomans, fireplace fenders, and sofas; you may be surprised just how many people you can seat. Buffets are generally more relaxed and the conversation more animated because people have more freedom of movement than they would at the dinner table, and can chat with others while standing in line to fill their plates. When it comes time for dessert, you have an opportunity to switch partners and possibly meet someone new. And, there is the matter of the menu. There are the no-carb eaters, the vegetarians, the gluten-free guests, and every once in awhile there is an old-fashioned carnivore who has seconds of the prime rib but will simply not eat anything green. This is when every guest is appreciative of the buffet format because no one feels bad about refusing food due to their restrictions—everyone gets exactly what they want!

If you like gathering people together, buffets are perfect for you.

M. F. K. Fisher distilled some guidelines for the buffet in a few sentences. "Plates should be large and easy to hold in one hand—no heavy porcelains—and they should have a well-defined edge or rim to take care of teeterings and swayings. In the same way, the silver should be light and simple, and the napkins should be large and, of course, never starched. Glasses, stemmed or not, should be short and solid."

Watermelon

When I saw a silk blouse printed with watermelon slices in a vintage shop in Los Angeles, I thought, "Now this has a future. . . . I'm just not sure exactly what that is. Give me a while." Anyone who shops, that is *hunts*, in vintage clothing stores knows that you will miss all the fun if you are not open-minded—if you do not let your eyes wander or be open to discoveries. More than once, I have coveted something that was either too small or too large, but it did not deter me from making a purchase because I knew I could have the piece altered or use it as inspiration to have a pattern created. I knew the moment I saw the watermelon blouse that it was going to have a happy afterlife.

After arriving home from Los Angeles I asked my housekeeper to very carefully take the blouse apart with a seam ripper. The pieces, freshly cleaned and pressed, were ready for scanning on the computer. Once it was scanned, we digitally pieced together the pattern. I said, "Tablecloth! It must be a tablecloth for Family Week." We created a new fabric to be produced digitally by enlarging the scale and creating a new repeat. I could now see my bright new tablecloth for an upcoming family gathering. After an afternoon of swimming and golf, what better backdrop for fried chicken and all the rest? Anyone can make his own fabric today with an iPhone or a digital camera. The possibilities are endless.

In the Sunroom

Our sunroom in the country has a round dining table that can accommodate six. For larger gatherings we use the dining room. There always seems to be one room in the house where everyone tends to gather; for some people it's the kitchen, others the family room; for ours, we always find ourselves in the sunroom. With windows on two sides, a fireplace, and a view to the living room and the garden we have a bead on what's happening everywhere.

Over the past year we winterized the room by adding windows and lining the walls with Portuguese tiles. This way, even in the winter, I feel like I am eating outside. The sunroom is the closest thing to dining alfresco and with the fireplace it takes the chill out of long New York winters.

> ## "*The simplest meal seems a gala affair when everyone is radiant and cheerful.*"
> — *JULIA REED*

> *"Show me another pleasure like dinner which comes every day and lasts an hour."*
> — CHARLES MAURICE DE TALLEYRAND

" *I've never heard of anyone being tired of lobster.* **"**

— JANE GRIGSON

From the Garden to the Table

Years ago when we renovated our kitchen in East Hampton, I took it a step further, naturally. Out of a long, wide hallway I created a flower room for arranging and for storing and displaying the vases and baskets I have collected over the years. I also had a couple of walls bumped out to create a breakfast area that almost sits in the kitchen garden.

Now, in the morning while having breakfast, I can look into the garden and sort out what I want to cut for bedside arrangements and the dinner table, in addition to simply enjoying the view. There are vases to select and fill for the living room, porch, and powder room. After making cuttings in the kitchen garden, I head to the rose garden and other borders to pluck what appeals.

The time spent cutting, walking, and thinking has a calming, almost meditative effect early in the morning. The act of trimming, conditioning, and arranging—and running back out for a little more lady's mantle, scented geranium, or a few long pieces of ivy—is when the real fun begins. At this juncture, fresh coffee in hand, I turn on the music, stare at my selection, and contemplate where to begin.

Blue & White

Ask any editor at a shelter magazine to name the color scheme that continues to be a perennial favorite, one that has stood the test of time. Your answer will almost certainly be blue and white. Whether a schoolboy's striped shirt or nautical blue cushions crisply trimmed in white, the reaction is similar. Fresh, crisp, clean, blue and white is a universal color language. In my travels to Portugal, Spain, Italy, France, and India the reactions to fountains, floors, walls, and ceilings executed in some permutation of blue and white—whether in elaborate mosaics, tiles, or murals—elicit the same response, the drawing in of breath, all in unison.

Blue-and-white Moroccan ceramics, APT and Chantilly china, and cobalt glasses find their way to my table every week. A collection of tablecloths in blue-and-white prints, accumulated over time, along with placemats embroidered with hydrangea and bluebells and more, give me plenty of opportunities to satisfy my own urge to decorate in blue and white, if only for the table.

Breakfast

Don't talk to me before I've had my coffee in the morning. I need to ease my way into the day at my own pace and I assume others do, too. That is why our guest rooms have their own coffee makers and refrigerators, so visitors can also start their day slowly, and at whatever hour.

Breakfast is the most important meal; it gets you going and can set the tone for the entire day. Our breakfast table is set the night before. It is such a nice way to be greeted in the morning, with a table ready and waiting. No work to do first thing—just fix the coffee, turn on the news, and peruse the headlines of the paper.

Please let me have my coffee first.

Moments in Between

One of the most important things you can do for yourself is to stop and take time out. I mean real time out, and only you know what works best. I call these the "moments in between," that is, the moments between obligations, between meetings and other commitments. However you choose to take time out and refresh yourself with coffee, tea, or maybe a glass of wine, take the time to make the environment just as pretty as the tables you set. Once you develop a rhythm taking time for yourself and capturing the moments in between, a funny thing begins to happen. Eventually, you will always want things done to that standard, you become more demanding, your eye will always look for ways to improve things, make your immediate environment more beautiful. Light the candles, pick up a beautiful napkin, and pour yourself a glass of wine. Just like entertaining others, it all begins with you.

THE
PLEASURE
OF YOUR
COMPANY

Parties simple, parties gargantuan — but always gay parties,
amusing parties, enjoyable parties. Above all, enjoyable. — M. F. K. FISHER

The *pleasure* of your company: what could be a nicer way of beginning an invitation? Your company and the pleasure of it all suggest one's willingness to put all aside, to open one's home, and to spend one's time focused on and caring for invited guests. For dinner, lunch, a cocktail party, or dessert after a concert, whatever it is, you have made a conscious decision to suspend all responsibilities and ready your rooms for fun. After a dinner party I gave this past summer one of my guests wrote me a note saying how much she enjoys coming to our house for dinner because it really is a dinner *party*, not just a dinner. A nuance, I agree, but to me that was the highest compliment because it was a statement about the atmosphere. A good meal a cook can make; knowing where to go for wine advice can produce a brilliant selection; and any number of floral designers can produce some floral magic, but atmosphere speaks to the host/hostess.

In her book *Entertaining with Elegance*, Geneviève Antoine Dariaux expresses her opinion on numerous aspects of hostessing and entertaining. With imagination, organization, and the right attitude she felt every woman could learn to be a confident hostess. Further, if you are to create a hospitable atmosphere, you must first "express warmth, friendliness, refinement and graciousness in your daily life, week after week, year after year." Getting a certain rhythm in your entertaining requires some practice. Start now, select a date, make a list of people, and begin like this: "The pleasure of your company . . ."

Caftan Caucus

I can credit my friend Deb Shriver with having come up with a name for a girls' weekend I have in East Hampton every summer. As the invited group stood around talking one summer we looked at each other, all in caftans, and Deb proclaimed, "Well, this is a caftan caucus if I've ever seen one." The name just stuck.

On Thursday night of that weekend I have a dinner party for my houseguests and other girlfriends. The conversation is animated; future plans are made; and the laughter can be deafening. A time to catch up, swim, read, walk on the beach, and talk until the wee hours. There is absolutely no agenda for this caucus; however, there might be one goal, to leave more relaxed than you arrived. What every hostess prays for.

Caftan Caucus
July 21st, 2016

Baharat Spiced Chilled Yellow Squash Soup

Coconut-Lemongrass-Cardamom Grilled Chicken
with Green Peppercorn- Cucumber Yogurt Sauce

Cold Lobster Salad in Bibb Lettuce Cups
with Green Goddess Dressing

Multicolor Carrot Ribbon Salad with Baby Arugula

Corn and Sweet Red Bell Pepper Fritters

Cold Cherry Soufflé

Ramey Chardonnay, 2011
Williams Selyem, Pinot Noir 2013
Pierre Moncuit Champagne

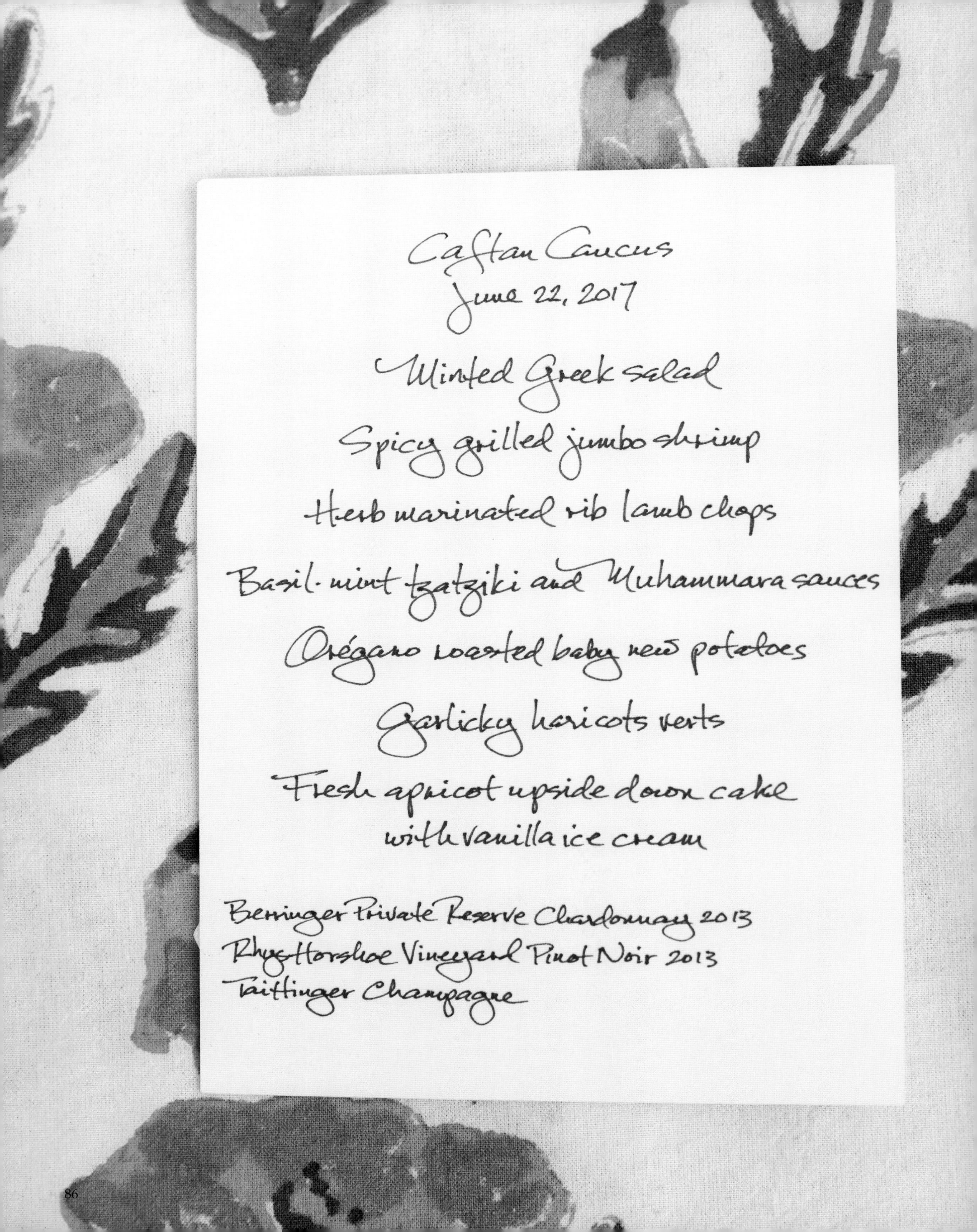

Caftan Caucus
June 22, 2017

Minted Greek salad

Spicy grilled jumbo shrimp

Herb marinated rib lamb chops

Basil-mint tzatziki and Muhammara sauces

Orégano roasted baby new potatoes

Garlicky haricots verts

Fresh apricot upside down cake
with vanilla ice cream

Beringer Private Reserve Chardonnay 2013
Rhys Horshoe Vineyard Pinot Noir 2013
Taittinger Champagne

Caftan Caucus
July 9, 2015

Cold Carrot-Ginger and Tomato Cardamom Soups
with a Coriander Cream Garnish

•

Grilled Vadouvan Chicken Skewers

•

Goan Curried Coconut Shrimp

•

Poppadums

•

Spiced Baby Pat Squash

•

Saffron Spiced Rice Pulao

•

Spicy Tomato Chutney

•

Narial Chatni (Coconut-Coriander Chutney)

•

Saffron-Rosewater Ice Cream with
Pistachio Cake

Ramey Chardonnay 2011
Brittan Vineyards, Pinot Noir 2010
Schramsberg Blanc de Noirs

Summer Nights

August is a big month for entertaining our friends. There are always lunches and a number of dinner parties. Mark Sanne and I work on menus a couple months in advance. I design the table setting to be compatible with the menu, have place cards done in calligraphy, and sort out what flowers I will use in the living room, the sunroom, and elsewhere.

Cocktails are always on the terrace, weather permitting, and the bar and the terrace dining table are also decorated. I generally select a group of topiaries, several pots of maidenhair ferns, or a simple splash of color with a row of glorious pale pink geraniums. All speak to the house and the season.

I want my guests to be relaxed, yet at the same time I want them to feel special, to feel entertained, and to know it is all being done for them. Summer nights should be memorable.

8·17·17

Steamed baby carrot and orange salad
with micro greens and
orange-ginger-mint dressing

Chicken and apricot tangine

Herbed saffron and pistachio pilaf

Swiss chard with preserved lemons

Frozen plum hibiscus soufflés
with fruit

Château Pichon Lalande 2000
Jean-marc Pillot Puligny Montrachet 2010
Pierre Moncuit Blanc de Blanc

8·22·17

Melon, tomato and feta salad in a baby melon

Herb, garlic and lemon marinated
grilled lamb chops
Minted yogurt sauce

Roasted swordfish with
Kalamata olives, capers and roasted tomatoes

Stuffed tomatoes with spinach and haloumi

Grilled eggplant with yogurt tahini and
pomegranate seeds

Pistachio cake with
roasted figs and pomegranate syrup

Château Ducru Beaucaillou 2000
Jean-marc Pillot Puligny Montrachet 2010
Laurent Perrier Champagne

Charleston

The final stop of my Southern road trip was Charleston, South Carolina.

My friend Susan Hull Walker gave a dinner party for me and Jane Scott Hodges in her beautiful garden, complete with an Indian menu, a cocktail prepared for the evening, a table decorated in deep turquoise, and beautiful embroidered Indian lanterns hanging from the trees. The scent of jasmine that blanketed her bannister wafted through the garden.

Susan—the owner of Ibu, a company that works with over seventy artisan groups operated by women in approximately thirty countries—has a global approach to life, her decorating, her wardrobe, and her entertaining. Because caftans are a part of her trade, she made them required dress for the evening. It was a beautiful night with everyone in a festive mood and looking terribly glam.

Book Party

One look at the acknowledgments in most books and you will see a list of names that fill a page. Writers, photographers, stylists, art directors, editors, great friends, assistants, house managers, housekeepers, cooks, gardeners, on and on. *Garden Inspirations,* my last book, was no exception. Once the book was in hand, a celebration was planned for friends and those involved with the project at Zezé Flowers, one of the prettiest shops in New York and a fitting location. A long banquet table was covered with one of my fabrics from Fabricut, and glassware, flatware, and linens were brought from home. No flowers were needed on the table, because they surrounded us; so maidenhair ferns mixed with hellebores made a frothy low hedge down the center of the table. After dinner: a surprise dessert that reflected the theme of the book! Each guest was presented with his or her own individual cake made for us by the incredible Sylvia Weinstock.

12 May 2015

Heirloom Tomatoes with Burrata

Cold Poached Salmon
Sauce Verte
White and Green Asparagus
and Corn Salad

Dessert... surprise!

Lewis Cellars Chardonnay, Sonoma 2013
Walter Scott Pinot Noir, Freedom Hill,
Willamette Valley 2012
Walter Scott Pinot Noir,
Sojouner Vineyard, Eola Amity 2013
Pol Roger Champagne Brut Reserve, NV

C·A·M

Cold yellow and red roasted pepper soup
with pumpkin seed oil

Oven roasted local halibut
on a bed of puréed fresh fava beans
Butter braised
French breakfast radishes

Warm local organic strawberries
with extra Vecchio balsamic
and black pepper

NEWTON CHARDONNAY
SEA SMOKE TEN PINOT NOIR 2014

NEW YORK CITY BALLET
SPRING GALA 2012
À La Française

THURSDAY, MAY 10

White and Green Asparagus
Shaved Black Truffles with Lemon Mousseline

Poussin à l'Orange
Baby Spring Vegetables
Potato Nests with Pommes Anna

Assortment of ...

Ballet Gala

I have co-chaired several galas for the New York City Ballet over the years. The number of details and moving parts are many, somewhat like a military maneuver, and thankfully the company's office handles them brilliantly. Keeping the gala dinner simple, elegant, and delicious can be a challenge for such a large group. That is why it is critical to work with a caterer that you can rely on and that understands your event, your guests, and you. Glorious Food in New York has been my go to for over twenty-five years. The same holds true for the event designer—here DeJuan Stroud is scheming with me and my co-chair, Marie Nugent-Head. Preparation for a dinner party at home takes the same eye for detail, just smaller in scale. Creating a beautiful backdrop and seating and feeding eight hundred people give one all the confidence needed to do it for twelve at home.

A Friend's First Book Party

While this is my tenth book, I remember all the details surrounding the publication of my first one: the commitments, the travel, the interviews, and first and foremost the sense of accomplishment and the excitement of it all. That is why it is my pleasure to help friends celebrate and launch their books.

When P. Gaye Tapp released her first book, *How They Decorated*, this past year—I was honored to have written the foreword—I gave a dinner to celebrate her. A fellow Southerner, albeit with a more pronounced accent, I knew she would appreciate a Southern-style buffet dinner. And luckily we had a beautiful evening for cocktails in the garden.

Mark Sanne, our chef, knows that when it comes to buffets guests will more often than not have seconds of his yummy corn pudding, succotash, some Smithfield ham, crab cakes, and his unforgettable coconut cake.

Dinner
in Celebration of
Gage Tapp + How They Decorated

Shrimp with andouille

Baked grits soufflé

Cumin rubbed pork tenderloin with
mostarda di frutta

Lemon crab salad

Fiddlehead ferns with
Meyer lemon vinaigrette

Mark's succotash

Hoe cakes + Pimento cheese

Coconut layer cake

Fresh strawberries with
Grand Marnier and orange zest

Harvest Dinner

It just happened to be Halloween the night I gave my friend Nina Campbell a small dinner party in New York. Because Nina lives in London and lands in New York frequently but for only a few days each time, I thought I would collect a group of girls that she otherwise might not have seen on such a short visit.

Setting the scene in the foyer, the tole lavabo was filled with miniature white pumpkins. On the commode in the gallery on the way to the dining room, I placed a vase filled with large orange Chinese lanterns. That same color scheme was repeated in the dining room with bittersweet vines and russet-colored chrysanthemums trailing down the center of the table and wrapping gilt-bronze candlesticks with ebony candles.

Courses were served alternately on basalt and creamware plates. For dessert Sylvia Weinstock made cakes in the shape of pumpkins with each guest's initials. Trick or treat.

October 31, 2016

Spicy pumpkin soup

Braised lamb shanks with
anchovies, lemon and herbs

Roasted cauliflower
with dukkah
Sautéed mustard greens

Dessert surprise

Ladoucette Pouilly-Fumé
Château La Gaffelière Grand Cru

Changing Seasons

Right after Labor Day everything seems to shift to a different gear. Fashion Week explodes on the New York scene, a new ballet season opens, the flowers in the market take on different hues, and you take one look in your closet and say, "It's time for a change." And so it goes on the home front. Summer slipcovers are retired to the linen closet for next year, and I start thinking about winter entertaining. A different palette shifts to the front of the linen drawers, the bamboo flatware is removed to a different silver closet, and the fragile hand-painted glasses with flowers are replaced by more of my favorites from William Yeoward.

Winter is upon us, so dust off your favorite pewter vase and your tole chinoiserie cachepot and start creating new table stories for your family, your friends, and yourself. A new season welcomes new opportunities for the table.

C·A·M

Veal and wild mushroom stew

Pumpkin gnocchi

Sautéed broccoli rabe
with garlic

Apple tart with crème fraîche

WILLIAM FEVRE CHABLIS BOUGROS 2014
CHÂTEAU KIRWAN MARGAUX 2005

C·A·M

Fennel, red onion and
blood orange salad with mâche

Pappardelle with chicken, black olives,
capers, feta and tomatoes

Roasted fresh figs, fresh ricotta
and chestnut honey
Almond tuiles

ANTINORI CERVARO DELLA SALA 2014
SASSICAIA 2013

Christmas Traditions

New York is a bustling place at Christmas. Helping clients with gift ideas and advising them on getting their houses ready for the holidays are part of the job. Christmas parties; gifts to buy, wrap, and deliver; organizing holiday charity donations; and packing for Aspen, where we go every year—all of this must be done in a highly organized way. How do I manage? In a word, spreadsheets.

In the midst of all the excitement, I have my annual Christmas buffet for as many girls as my living room and library can handle. I do not do a Christmas tree in New York since most of the holiday is spent in Colorado. The front of our town house and the garden pergola with its fireplace are the two areas that get decorated and set the tone for the season.

Years ago I decided to weave the railings of our iron fence and gate with red willow I had seen in large bundles at the flower market. I came home with a bundle to experiment with, all the while knowing that I would call Charlie Baker, a wood artist who has done work for me in East Hampton. Charlie wove the willow branches through the railings— and they're still like that almost six years later. At Christmastime we add garlands of greens across the top, and pray for an atmospheric dusting of snow. I schedule my luncheon for a Friday because some out-of-town guests stay for the weekend.

Party preparations include many conversations with Mark, who I've made an honorary Southerner because I know he has prepared enough Southern fare to qualify. Each year I select a graphic for the invitation that speaks to the season. I send these out by Paperless Post, because it's so efficient. In October I usually start thinking about a parting gift for my guests.

As some guests begin to drift out the door, others settle in for an afternoon of more laughs, conversation, champagne, and perhaps another go at Mark's unforgettable coconut cake.

Christmas Luncheon · December 16, 2016

Carved Smithfield country ham
Pear-cranberry chutney

Mark's crab cakes
Sauce russe

Chicken and wild mushroom fricassé with sherry

Baked wild and white rice with dried cranberries

Oven roasted yellow and red grape tomatoes with rosemary

Celery root, bell pepper and carrot remoulade

Sautéed shredded Brussels sprouts with crispy bacon and
pomegranate molasses

Silver dollar buttermilk biscuits

Homemade Pimento cheese

White birch Bûche de Noël
Assorted sugar cookies
Chocolate truffles

ROSEMARY'S VINEYARD PINOT NOIR TALLEY, 2014
RAMEY CHARDONNAY

If I could not get to the place, could I not, at least,
recapture the rapture of some faraway place? — *LESLEY BLANCH*

Long story short, a road trip through the South has always been a bucket list item of mine. Several years ago at a girls' dinner in East Hampton I asked everyone at the end of dinner if they would mind sharing something on their bucket list. As we went around the table, the reveals were amazing, and the conversations that ensued went on after midnight. When it was my turn, I announced that seeing the South, preferably in an RV, was high on my list.

Longing to channel Charles Kuralt, the following year I blocked out a week on my calendar six months in advance so that I could explore a piece of my native South, meeting with craftsmen, artists, and chefs along the way. I started in Richmond, Virginia, my hometown. There I spent a day seeing things I had not seen in years. The next day I picked up my friend and traveling partner Jane Scott Hodges at the airport and we headed to Williamsburg, our first stop. We had appointments with curators at historic houses such as Westover and Berkeley plantations, and Upper Shirley.

After winding our way across Virginia, we stopped in Greensboro to see a children's museum with an edible garden. After visiting Caroline Faison Antiques and the Pink Door Antiques, we headed straight to Blackberry Farm in Tennessee. More on that later.

Several cities later, including an afternoon at Biltmore Estate, we made our way to Charleston, the scheduled wrap of our trip, where we had a full schedule.

From a generation that remembers Dinah Shore "seeing the USA in your Chevrolet" . . . and Charles Kuralt providing Americans with glimpses of the back roads and the spirited people that lived there, I knew this would be my maiden voyage in a vehicle exploring the landscape I have flown over for so many years.

Four star hotels; country inns; back road discoveries; meeting and talking to great chefs, an ebullient sommelier, and knowledgeable gardeners—all added immeasurably to the experience of travel.

Good Morning

...wnstairs to the breakfast table is exercise enough fo...

Chauncey Mitchell Depew (1834–1928)

Charlotte

Monticello

My first visit to Monticello was as a fourth grader, our first class trip on a bus. Growing up in Richmond we were blessed with historic sites to visit, and Monticello was always spoken about with a certain reverence. I remember that I bought my mother a Claire Burke fragrance in the gift shop on that trip. Fond memories. Fast forward: now, I am a trustee of the foundation that is responsible for its care, its mission, its future. I view my role there as an honor and a privilege, and I value what I have learned from my fellow trustees.

One year in November, I was asked to be the guest editor in chief of *House Beautiful*. Sorting out the stories for my issue, I offered Monticello as a backdrop for a feature on creating table settings with modern tableware within a historic landmark, demonstrating the ease of mixing old with new, antique with modern, monochrome with bursts of color.

161

> *The power of gathering: It inspired us, delightfully. To be more hopeful, more joyful, more thoughtful: in a word, more alive.*
> — ALICE WATERS

Ditchley

A couple years ago I organized a trip to England with Margot Shaw, publisher of *Flower* magazine. The trip was organized around a stay at Ditchley Park, with visits to Kelmarsh Hall and Haseley Court, the residences of Nancy Lancaster. Lectures in the evening before dinner, private tours, dinner in the saloon—all furthered our knowledge of the expat who helped put the English Country House look on the map along with her partner John Fowler.

Nancy, a Virginian by birth, embraced the arts of fine living and instinctively created elegance with comfort. Visiting the houses, walking the gardens, embracing the color palettes, and hearing the stories about Nancy filled in between the lines of what had been previously written about her. There is no substitute for being there and capturing a sense of place.

21 May 2015

Salad of Parma ham and fresh figs with
Oxford blue cheese

Breast of white Cotswold chicken with a
Chicken Boudin
Pearl barley and spring vegetables

Cheese course

Mini Pavlova with passion fruit

Coffee or mint tea
Selection of truffles and macaroons

POUILLY-FUISSÉ 'TERRORIS DE FUISSÉ',
  SELECTION CHRISTOPHE CORDIER 2012

CHÂTEAU SÉNÉJAC, CRU BOURGOIS,
  HAUT-MÉDOC 2010

COCKBURN'S VINTAGE PORT 1985

PAUL ROGER RÉSERVE NV

"Glorious England"
The Nancy Lancaster Legacy
(Charlotte Moss Group)
Wednesday 20th May to Friday 2...

Ballyfin

In the past two years, I have been to Ballyfin in Ireland three times and I long for my next visit. After a Scottish train excursion with my husband, I wanted to go to a place where we could unwind: a quiet place to walk in the country, shoot some skeet, read books for hours, and have a beautiful dinner every night. The answer was Ballyfin. The restoration of this Irish country house is impeccable; the decoration elegant, comfortable, cozy, and inviting; the service spot on; the food excellent and locally sourced. For lunch one afternoon we reserved the Picnic House, on a slight rise through the woods and overlooking the hills toward Dublin. When we arrived in our golf cart, the fire was ablaze; the table, with checked cloth and silver, was set with the meal we had preordered and a surprise from a client—a bottle of Dom Pérignon on ice. We spent time there collapsed in wicker chairs warmed by the sun and still laughing over moments from our train trip—a glorious day.

"Eating outdoors makes for good health and long life and good temper, everyone knows that.

— *JULIA REED*

> *Live in each season as it passes, breathe the air,*
> *drink the drink, taste the fruit,*
> *and resign yourself to the influence of the earth.*
> — HENRY DAVID THOREAU

La Vieux Logis

When touring gardens in the Dordogne region of France several years ago, we stayed at Le Vieux Logis near Trémolat. I made a plan to alternate days we spent touring with days to relax and make notes. I did not want to wear out my husband; after all, this was a vacation.

Le Vieux Logis was the perfect choice, with a Michelin-rated restaurant and a beautiful outside dining area under sculpted plane trees. Our view from the chaise lounges by the pool on those alternative days was an allée and a lawn punctuated with boxwood balls of different sizes in a random pattern. Every night we ate under the trees, where the tables were set in an all white scheme and lit by candles—simple, elegant perfection.

A Paris Treat

On the way back from a trip to Florence I stopped in Paris for a few days of seeing museums and shopping for clients. I took a friend to meet Eric Goujou, owner of La Tuile à Loup, one of my favorite shops, which specializes in ceramics made by French artisans. Eric works with and finds artists creating unique decorative pieces as well as dinnerware.

Eric is always receptive to custom orders and experimenting with color combinations. I have worked with him on many beautiful pieces for clients and myself.

When we arrived at his shop, a spread was laid out for us. What better way to see it all and work on new orders than with a glass of champagne?

Castel Monastero

Castel Monastero, a former country house and hunting lodge of the Chigi Saracini family, is now a luxury hotel in the heart of Tuscany near Siena. Every morning my husband, Barry, and I enjoyed breakfast in the sunny courtyard shaded by large white umbrellas. Each day the breakfast buffet was set up beautifully, and each time it was a little different—the arrangement of glass vessels, handwoven baskets, pristine white linens, a tall ceramic vase filled with country flowers. All details were noted.

There is much to be enjoyed and learned at the tables of a great hotel—to be beautiful *and* efficient is an accomplishment. How often do you find inspiration and ideas from your travels? I am always taking notes and photos, for ideas, inspiration, and improvement.

Florence

I have been lucky in my life to have clients who share my enthusiasm for setting the table, entertaining their friends, and hunting for unique items to accomplish those goals. One of my clients recently restored an apartment in a beautiful palazzo on the Arno with stunning views of Florence. Needless to say, while there, every meal was taken on the loggia watching the light find its way over the rooftops, down the river, through the narrow streets, and finally illuminating the Duomo.

A study in green, this particular table setting reflects her sensibility and playfulness. During my visit, not one setting was repeated. We made a visit to Richard Ginori to see the beautiful store there and to see what was new. Because, after all, a girl cannot own enough plates.

The Train

A significant wedding anniversary was approaching, and my husband asked, "What would you like to do?" After some research and a few phone calls, we decided to see Scotland on the Belmond Royal Scotsman. Neither of us really knew the Scottish countryside or had taken a train trip together and felt it would be an adventure, and it was. Long story short, it was the smallest space we have ever been in together and we laughed until we cried over various incidents. At the same time, the staff was amazing, the food delicious, and the tables beautifully set every night for black tie dinners. One afternoon I chatted with the young man who was responsible for folding the napkins for our dinners. I complimented his work, and told him he would make Carson proud. He laughed but beamed as he said, "Thank you, there are so many ways to fold them you know." Yes, I know, thanks for the reminder.

"*Dining, like theater, requires a glorious set.*"
— ANONYMOUS

Blackberry Farm

My Southern road trip included a much-awaited visit to Blackberry Farm, an American treasure and luxury resort and the westernmost point on our itinerary. In two short days my friend Jane and I hiked each morning, went canoeing after breakfast, took a cooking class, waded through a wine list of a cellar that boasts 50,000 bottles (luckily with help from the sommeliers), and dined with Kreis Beall, founder and director of design.

One day for lunch we had a picnic in the boathouse, which is perched on the edge of the pond with the most spectacular views of the Smoky Mountains. This was a shoulder-dropping moment to be savored as we sunk back into two Adirondack chairs. Later, as we set the table, we both laughed as both of us brought linens for the trip. Leave nothing to chance.

Room Service

Just the words "room service" suggest something luxurious, don't they? Whether I am on a holiday or a business trip, I much prefer room service to getting dressed to go to a dining room. The solitude of my own room, and doing something on my own time, is one of life's great luxuries. I have photos of room service trays from all over the world. There is a lesson, or a reminder, in everything.

If I am on the road and have an early start, the day begins in my room in peace, reading papers, watching the news, collecting my wits, and looking at the agenda for the day. To have the day begin this way somehow gives order and calm to the rest of it. At the same time, the way the tray is set with crisp linens and a single flower makes me feel like I am home. A dose of beauty to start the day always works.

Make your own brand of room service at home— what could be better?

ENTERTAINING LADIES

The very meaning of the word hospitable implies a disposition to welcome all guests, and indeed all comers, with generosity and warmth; based in temperament and personality it is, in part, the gift of putting the highest degree of attention to your guests before all personal considerations. —CONSTANCE SPRY

Confidence, generosity, and curiosity—fueled by enthusiasm and imagination—led all of the women in the following pages to the table, the place where they could share its bounty with style, ease, and grace. From diverse backgrounds they all found entertaining and collecting people as another expression of their styles. Each possessed the creativity, spontaneity, and joy of a real hostess, and each had the ability to rise to the occasion no matter what happened. What also unites them is the capacity *for imagination*. Imagination, coupled with an enormous desire to learn, enabled them to invent something unique, whatever their pocketbooks allowed at the time. Elsa Maxwell once engineered a fake heist with actors as policemen to liven up a party for her society guests. Guests of Lesley Blanch sat on the floor, a patchwork of oriental carpets, having a meal made from one of her cookbooks, compilations of dishes collected from her travels, while Marjorie Merriweather Post, the richest woman in America at the time, served JELLO for dessert on Franciscan Ware or a royal Russian dinner service, alike. Some cerebral, others effervescent, they all opened their homes and their lives to others while brightening the rooms they entered. Uplifting the lives of those in their orbit was part of their raison d'etre. Diana Vreeland called them "life enhancers" who all possessed a quality worth aspiring to. In a recent article for British *Vogue* Hayley Bloomingdale remembers her grandmother Betsy Bloomingdale, a couture-clad party giver, as "always dressed up when she was dressed down . . . nothing makes a special occasion more special than dressing up." Betsy herself would tell you, "There is no great secret to entertaining successfully. You can have all the money and the privilege in the world and possess no style. You can spend a fortune and leave your guests feeling bored and let down. Real style comes from within." All of the women here, I think, would agree that the most important thing is just to make a plan, get dressed, open the door, let the party begin, and be yourself—your best possible self.

Tuesday
Nov. 13, 1962
6:45 PM
10 persons

FAMILY DINNER

Creme Maryland

Filet Mignon St. Amand

Pommes Bucheronne

Salad Mimosa

Souffle Chocolat White House

Chateau Haut Brion 1955

Dom Perignon   1952

Pauline de Rothschild: The Creator

Pauline de Rothschild was shy, private, and transcendent. She was born with certain attributes: an unerring eye, a kindness for and interest in others, and a vast imagination for fantasy and the courage to carry it out. She more or less invented herself and the world she wanted, sharing her vision through entertainments as a legendary hostess.

She married into a great French family, and elevated it even further because she had something money cannot buy: intelligence and boundless curiosity. "She can dominate a room from a footstool," said her friend Diana Vreeland.

Her whimsy delighted her guests. Every morning, she selected her china, silver, tablecloths, and napkins from books that contained photographs and swatches of over one hundred seventy patterns. These were the raw materials she used to create the table landscapes she became famous for. She might create a fantastical forest down the center of the table, place ornamental kale in silver vases, or invent a miniature cherry orchard by putting branches in Japanese pots.

With her raffiné charm, Pauline brought her dreams to life.

Lesley Blanch: The Explorer

"I have always had a strong appetite for life and for loving."

If Lesley Blanch was anything, she was an adventurer. "Get up and get on with it," she proclaimed. Born in London in 1904, she seemed almost allergic to staying at home. Describing herself as a "scholarly romantic," she did many things well—painting, socializing, and writing, even working as a features editor at British *Vogue* on the eve of the Second World War. A bestselling author, she wrote a book *The Wilder Shores of Love* that has been in print since its first publication in 1954.

It was her ability to travel beyond what was expected of her that made her reputation. She fell in love with the Middle East and explored Turkey, North Africa, Outer Mongolia, Egypt, Iran, Samarkand, Afghanistan, and the Sahara when most women—or men—barely left their hometowns. She never stopped exploring.

When she turned 100, Lesley tried to answer the *why* of her ceaseless adventures. "I wanted to be moving towards color," she explained. Blanch lived to be 102; so clearly she was doing something right.

Bunny Mellon: The Collector

Rachel "Bunny" Mellon was born with a discerning eye and cultivated her own brand of good taste. A devoted gardener, she created a 4,000-acre oasis at Oak Spring Farm in Upperville, Virginia, as well as the Rose Garden at the White House, where her original design remains today.

As a collector, Bunny loved many things—vegetables fashioned in ceramic, Schlumberger objects and jewelry, and clothing designed for her by Balenciaga and Givenchy. Most importantly, however, the library she created at Oak Spring has become one of the most enviable horticultural collections in the world. She even helped design the building that would house her collection.

Bunny Mellon created her own world at Oak Spring in the gardens, the library, and her greenhouses. Her horticultural interests revealed themselves in every aspect of her life, including her china, her linens, and the objects she used to decorate the table.

Marjorie Merriweather Post: The Record Keeper

"Do whatever you want regardless of the planned activities offered,
and if there is anything you want and you don't ask for it, it's your own fault."

Marjorie Merriweather Post, whose $5 billion fortune came from cold cereal and frozen food, was one of the twentieth-century's great hostesses. With stunning residences in three states, and the *Sea Cloud*, a 316-foot yacht, Marjorie was an enviable chatelaine who made it all look easy, because she was disciplined, optimistic, energetic, and highly organized.

Marjorie was meticulous about record-keeping and thinking of every contingency—from documenting every Christmas gift she ever received to handing out heel protectors to female guests to safeguard wooden floors. For her dinner parties, butlers worked all day perfecting tables, using yardsticks to measure the precise placement of dinner plates, napkins, silver, and candleholders. At Hillwood, her property in Washington, D.C., the table settings included the Russian Imperial service, while at Topridge, her Adirondack camp, she used Copeland, Franciscan, and Staffordshire. As a hostess, she was generous beyond compare.

TUESDAY 16th JULY 1968.

LUNCHEON

SALAD

****

PORTERHOUSE STEAK

GRILLED TOMATOES & MUSHROOMS

EGG PLANT.BAKED POTATO.BROAD BEANS.

****

APPLE TAPIOCA PUDDING

****

DINNER

JELLIED CONSOMME

****

SADDLE OF LAMB
RED CURRENT & MINT SAUCE

BROCCOLI AU GRATIN,DUCHESS POTATOES,PUREE OF PEAS,

****

FRUIT JELLO RING,SHERBERT BALLS

****

Dinner - March 6 - 8:00 pm - 20 or 22 peop
at 8:45

arapes - 1) caviar ... til it is hard +
crisp.
2) raw veg

Course Cold s
Cucumb
Sauce a
w

ain course roast)watercress garnish
brown

Jacqueline Kennedy: The First Lady

"Housekeeping is a joy to me. I feel that this is what I was made for.
When it all runs smoothly, when the food is good and the flowers are fresh, I have such satisfaction."

Jacqueline Kennedy is one of the most influential First Ladies of the twentieth century. During her active life, her interests ran toward books, poetry, and horses—and *not* politics.

When it came to entertaining in the presidential style, Jacqueline Kennedy opted for round tables suitable for ease and conversation, rather than banqueting tables, which had long been the norm in the White House.

Flower arrangements for state dinners during this time are well documented, in words and in photographs. The morning after a dinner, members of the staff could expect a note written on yellow legal paper complimenting them on their efforts and the menu, and offering suggestions on what might get tweaked next time.

Write in blue Happy Birthday Matthias

Elsie de Wolfe: The Decorator

"Be pretty if you can, be witty if you must, but be gracious if it kills you!"

Peppy, five-foot-two dynamo Elsie de Wolfe spoke with a New York accent and exercised by standing on her head well into her seventies. She also was attributed with having invented interior decorating as we know it today. Zebra rugs, leopard prints, chintz, and painted furniture were just a few of her signature items. Until Elsie, they had never been used together in an American interior. She was a master hostess—throwing cocktail parties, showing movies at home (a first for 1926), and, ever the life of a party, often doing cartwheels.

Elsie invented what we call today "The Mix," combining the high and the low at her parties. Titled Europeans mingled with American tycoons, movie stars, well-born gigolos, fashion designers, and artists of all kinds.

Betsy Bloomingdale: The Ultimate Hostess

"Entertaining is not a frivolous endeavor; I believe it is one of the great essentials of life."

As a hostess, Betsy was known for her attention to detail—taking copious notes of each dinner party, including a photograph of the place setting, the menu, and her outfit, so guests would never have the same experience twice. Generally, she thought guests appreciated straightforward menus. Her own signature first course was caviar and smoked salmon with a dab of crème fraîche in half an avocado. She clipped dahlias from her garden and put them in vintage silver for her guests to enjoy. Bloomingdale insisted, however, that it was the people who made a party: "It's not what you put on the table, it's what you put in the chairs."

Although fastidious about entertaining, Betsy did not take herself too seriously. One friend described her as "a cross between Babe Paley and Lucille Ball." Her sense of fun was reflected in elegant peanut-butter-and-bacon hors d'oeuvres, which she served at every party. An energetic socializer, she was a great confidante. Known as the "First Friend" during the Reagan presidency, she counted Nancy Reagan, Lauren Bacall, Nan Kempner, and Cary Grant as friends.

Elsa Maxwell: The Party Animal

"Etiquette—a fancy word for simple kindness."

Elsa Maxwell could throw *a party*. She had neither looks nor pedigree, yet all of society bowed to her for an invitation to one of her outrageous soirées. Earls and dukes hobnobbed with Cole Porter and Marilyn Monroe at her events, which ranged from murder-mystery parties to barnyard-themed hoedowns on Park Avenue.

As the Duke of Windsor put it, "The old battering-ram Elsa gives the best parties." According to Elsa's own estimation, she threw over three thousand fetes, making international news from 1910 to the 1960s. And, her advice? "The best you can offer your guests is the unexpected."

Elizabeth David: The Champion of Home Cookery

"Good food is always a trouble and its preparation should be regarded as a labour of love."

Elizabeth David was Britain's first lady of food, leading English cooking from the grayness of postwar austerity to an exotic world of fresh lemons, herbs, and garlic. She was an evangelist for olive oil, good bread, and seasonal eating, even using fresh, not canned, tomatoes—unheard of in 1951.

She paved the way for future generations. Jamie Oliver, Nigella Lawson, and nearly every British cook you've ever heard about or watched is in her debt and will gladly admit it.

Pêches au vin banc (Peaches in white wine)

The best peaches for this dish are the yellow-fleshed variety.

Dip the fruit in boiling water so that the skins can easily be peeled off. Slice them straight into big wine glasses, sprinkle with sugar and pour a tablespoon or two of white wine into each glass. Don't prepare them too long ahead or the fruit will go mushy.

o

Poulet à l'estragon (Chicken with tarragon)

Tarragon is an herb which has quite remarkable affinity with chicken, and a poulet à l'estragon, made with fresh tarragon, is one of the great treats of the summer. There are any amount of different ways of cooking a tarragon-flavoured chicken dish: here is a particularly successful one.

For plump roasting chicken weighing about 2 lb. when plucked and drawn, knead a good ounce of butter with a tablespoon of tarragon leaves, half a clove of garlic, salt and pepper. Put this inside the bird, which should be well coated with olive oil. Roast the bird lying on its side on a grid in a baking dish. Turn it over a half-time (45 minutes together in a pretty hot oven or an hour in moderate oven should be sufficient; those who have a roomy grill might try grilling it, which takes about 20 minutes, and gives much more the impression of a spit-roasted bird, but it must be constantly watched and turned over very carefully, so that the legs are as well done as the breast).

When the bird is cooked, heat a small glass of brandy in a soup ladle, set light to it, pour it flaming over the chicken and rotate the dish so that the flames spread and continue to burn as long as possible. Return the bird to a low oven for 5 minutes, during which time the brandy sauce will mature and lose its raw flavor. At this moment you can, if you like, enrich the sauce with a few spoonfuls of thick cream and, at La Mère Michele's Paris restaurant, from where the recipe originally came, they add Madeira to the sauce. Good though this is, it seems to me a needless complication.

o

Zuppa di fagioli alla toscasna (Tuscan bean soup)

½ lb. of white beans, parsley, garlic, salt and pepper, olive oil.

Put the previously soaked bean to cook, covered with 3 pints of water. When they are tender (about 3 hours) put half the beans through a sieve and return the resulting purée to the rest of the beans in the pan. Season with salt and pepper. In a little olive oil heat the chopped garlic (the quantity depends entirely upon individual taste) and add a good handful of chopped parsley. Stir this mixture into the soup, and before serving add a little fresh olive oil.

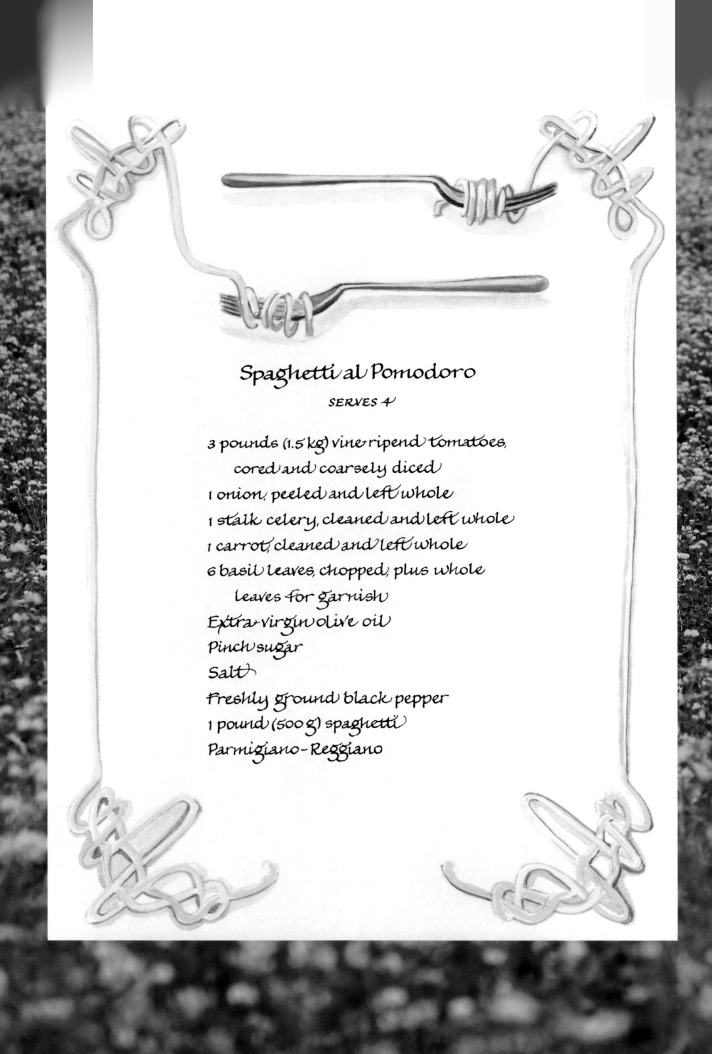

Spaghetti al Pomodoro

SERVES 4

3 pounds (1.5 kg) vine-ripend tomatoes,
   cored and coarsely diced
1 onion, peeled and left whole
1 stalk celery, cleaned and left whole
1 carrot, cleaned and left whole
6 basil leaves, chopped, plus whole
   leaves for garnish
Extra-virgin olive oil
Pinch sugar
Salt
Freshly ground black pepper
1 pound (500 g) spaghetti
Parmigiano-Reggiano

Audrey Hepburn: Mother First

"It's the flowers you choose, the music you play, the smile you have waiting . . ."

Audrey Hepburn is widely known as a famous movie star, but her dream in life was to be a wife and mother first. After the Second World War, she wanted a peaceful, settled home life.

Onscreen, she was glamorous and elegant and dressed in Givenchy. At home at *La Paisible*, her sanctuary in Switzerland, she was relaxed and playful, leaving her public life behind.

Audrey loved being a mother. She cooked, entertained friends, gardened, went for long walks, and spent time with her two boys, Sean and Luca—in contrast to her onscreen persona, usually outfitted in jeans, a polo shirt, and sneakers. During the boys' school years in Rome, she walked them to school everyday.

Today, Audrey is remembered for her humanitarianism and her own brand of Hollywood glamour. To those who were close to her, she is remembered as an amazing mother and friend.

Details, details, details, those distinguishing elements that set us all apart. Everything you do is an opportunity to put your own personal stamp on something in order to call it your own. Why wouldn't you seize every opportunity? Maybe you can recall moments as a child when you insisted on doing something your own way. Perhaps you've never let up. I have always had opini ons about things since I was old enough to look at colors and put together the ones I thought went together, or to know whether a blouse went with a certain skirt. I was the oldest of five, go figure.

Decorating houses professionally for over thirty-two years has enabled me to help guide others in developing their own voice, to develop their own opinions, their own style. It is not the broad strokes, the big decisions, in decorating that necessarily set us apart, but those telling details that distinguish one home from the next. The arrangement of furniture, how art is hung, the shape and materials of the lampshades, the layering of rugs or waxed wooden floors, the way windows are covered or not. Above and beyond, all of the furniture, art, and objects reflect how we live in the place we call home, and how we celebrate every day there. Never one to shy away from an opportunity to do some decorating, I have embraced doing it every day by setting my table. The china, the linens, the flatware, a single blossom, a small nosegay, or a potted fern—all of these elements give us a chance to decorate every day, to express ourselves through the details and to make every day an occasion.

Linens

For linens, as with china, my eyes are always peeled for new ideas, colors, and patterns for myself and my clients. Linens allow you to personalize your table, and for less of an investment than your china. Changing the colors and patterns of your linens with your china creates new stories every time you set the table. Keeping it simple on a daily basis doesn't mean it has to be the same everyday. Changing it up not only enhances the look of the table but also adds a sense of anticipation about the next meal—another opportunity to create beauty.

Whether you are all about linens in pure white, in solid hot colors, patterned, or strictly embroidered, the possibilities are endless as are the combinations. Every day you have a chance to decorate your table; and by embracing this idea and putting it into practice, over time you will unknowingly do it with ease and confidence. For years I have been mixing antique white napkins with everything I own, and will be doing it for years to come. As I said earlier, buying a beautiful set of white napkins for your linen closet will be the foundation to your collection, if you are so inclined. You have to start somewhere, so let it begin here. Before long you will find yourself eyeing variations on the theme, or branching out for something new altogether—I guarantee it.

66 *I'd rather not eat than eat off an ugly plate.* **99**

—*VALENTINO*

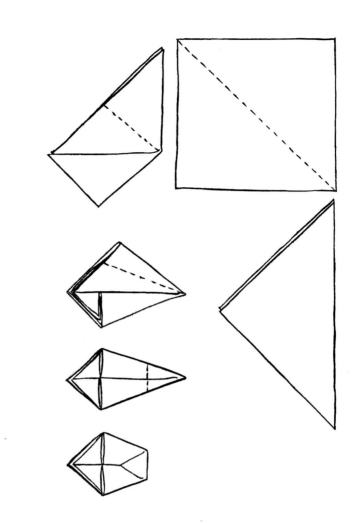

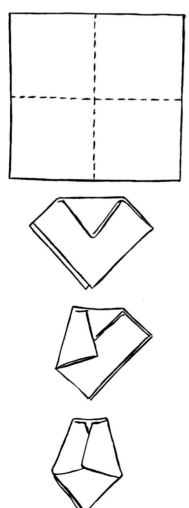

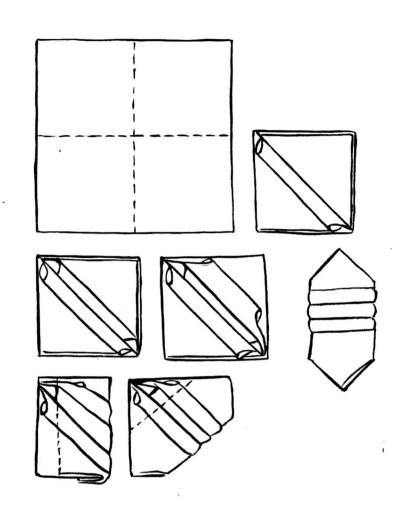

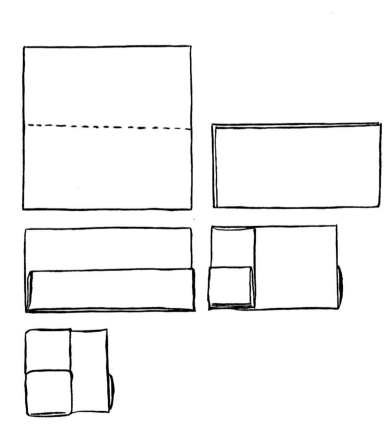

Flowers & Centerpieces

A single blossom, a big colorful bouquet, a blooming plant, a small topiary—any and all can help decorate and enliven a room. When it comes to the table, a centerpiece can inspire or complete your scheme.

Today we are blessed with sections in the supermarket devoted to flowers, sidewalk flower shops, roadside stands during growing season, and of course, your favorite florist or local nursery. Big stores often have outdoor gardening centers with potted plants, lots of annuals, and always something you didn't know you needed! I love those surprises. I have repeatedly said, "If you are a little reluctant to make an arrangement, then buy a bundle of one flower. Focus on the shape and fullness but make it generous." I prefer to see a mass of daisies, carnations, or other inexpensive flower than an expensive vase of exotica.

In lieu of flowers, I have used objects, such as a lidded tureen, bowls of seashells, a grouping of topiaries, or small stacks of gardening books of various sizes for a luncheon with fellow gardeners. Shop your closets.

How to get ideas? How to get started? What kind of flowers will work with my china? Can I mix country flowers with a formal setting? I tell everyone—my clients, anyone that asks, everyone at my lectures, anyone who will listen—to just tear out photos from magazines, take photos wherever you go, look at Instagram and Pinterest, and of course, buy books! All of these sources will inform your process, give you ideas to experiment with, fine-tune your eye, and boost your confidence.

> *Place a bouquet of flowers on the table and everything will taste twice as good.*
>
> — MICHAEL POLLAN

Place Cards

A designated seat at a meal is one of the many elements of a party that sets the scene. Show that you made the extra effort and thoughtfully considered the best seat for each guest.

Tented place cards are available in a variety of colors and designs. You can handwrite them yourself or have them calligraphed, but please no typing!

When it comes to placement, mix up the bankers with the ballerinas, artists with lawyers, media moguls with yoga instructors. Whether a seated dinner or a buffet with table seating, get out your Post-it notes. Put a name on each one and move them around until you hear yourself say, "Perfect, I've got it."

66 *The effect of effortless spontaneity often requires extensive planning.* 99
— RUSSELL PAGE

China

Let me just say from the outset: I have accumulated a fair amount of china in my life, therefore I will make no apologies for my cache. I have only two bits of advice for you on this front. Find a set of white china to call your own, and keep adding to it—it will serve you well. When it comes to pattern, your reaction must be visceral. You must love it; you must want to eat off of it; buy things to go with it, linens, a centerpiece; you must be excited about it. That excitement will prompt invitations to be sent, for dinners and lunches. What could be better?

As a retailer, I was always searching for antique sets to mix with new stock. As a decorator, I have designed dinner services for my clients, searched for complete antique services, helped to round out one of their collections, or in a moment of excitement with an Italian workshop, bought them something they didn't even know they wanted—until it arrived, then they promptly planned a dinner around it. Setting the table is everyday decorating. Why not have fun with it?

Acknowledgments

Where to begin . . .

Kimberly Power made this book happen. As my assistant, she has juggled the day to day, all of my travel, my lectures, every event, dinner party, and luncheon; she managed our move to a new office and has stepped into decorating, helping me source and work with some vendors on special bespoke projects. Highly organized and putting everything on spreadsheets (my years on Wall Street still guide us), she is always one step ahead of me. Thank you for all of that and more—without you this book would be scheduled for 2019!

Ali Power, Kimberly's sister, my editor at Rizzoli for several previous books came to work with us this summer between graduate school and a new career. Ali helped us to speed things up and was another invaluable and crucial guiding voice.

Philip Reeser, my editor, with great patience, rarely saw me as Kimberly was running interference and representing me when I was on a plane to elsewhere.

Dina Dell'Arciprete, designer of five of my books, gives me a visual voice, takes the writing and the photographs, gives the mélange her practiced eye, and whirls it through her computer to produce the beautiful pages that at some point become a book.

Charles Miers, my publisher, always trusting, forever patient, encouraging with razor-sharp vision and insight. One word from Charles sometimes sets me on a different path, redirects my thinking, or prompts me to edit something that instinctively I knew I should have.

Gary Bohan has managed our house in East Hampton for sixteen years. He has seen me through many books and all the dinners and lunches documented within them. Gary has been a partner through the process—assisting with photography shoots, making props with me, visiting countless garden centers to find something particular that I had in mind, and helping me set and reset the table countless times.

Jeimmy Gonzalez, our housekeeper in East Hampton, not only looks over the house but also assists Gary at all meals, sets the table, and knows exactly how many plates are in a set, how many of each napkin I own, and when I need to replace anything. We have quite a few tablecloths, and Jeimmy knows which ones fit which table in the dining room, or on the porch or terrace. Jeimmy oversees all with Gary, so our summers are seamless and I can go about working on my books . . . with their help, of course.

Jasmin Rojas is the whiz at ironing, and she does volumes of it. Because I use linens for all meals, Jasmin has her work cut out for her and she does it beautifully. Everything has its place, and she knows exactly where that is.

Linda Galvis is Jeimmy's mom and assists her in taking care of the house—shopping and often cooking meals. Everyone pitches in when I am shooting for the book. I know they think I must be mad sometimes, but by now, they just roll with it.

Andreea Coman-Morris manages our New York town house, along with Wilma Liebman and Mai Gaudette. They have created inventories of china and silver (and everything else, I think), and maintain them beautifully, understanding how important setting the table is to me. I hope that when they go about setting the table when I am at work, they have some fun in the process, experimenting with new combinations. I can tell that they are proud of what they do, and we appreciate it all.

Good parties do not just happen. There's a lot of preplanning and a team of great people. The team in our houses includes a group of gentlemen that make it all happen, and seamlessly: Alex Bushuyev, Edward Campbell, Anthony Channing, Andre Gontijo, Allen Huie, Michael Jackson, Ross Norton, George Pappas, Edgar Rosales, Kestis Stonys, and Karl Wittman. They have all been working with me for years—serving at all of our parties, dinners, and lunches. We are lucky to have a group that gets along, has lots of experience working together in my houses, and knows where everything is. I am grateful for their loyalty, and for the fact that they now know what cocktail Mr. X prefers, who only drinks white wine, and who always wants to take home coconut cake at Christmas. Most importantly, apropos to the chat about a relaxed hostess, with the experience and preparedness of all of these people I can come down five minutes before guests are due to arrive, have a quick whiz around, order a glass of champagne, and be ready when the doorbell rings. It doesn't get any better than that.

Mark Sanne has been cooking for and satisfying the appetites of my family for over twenty-four years. From Family Week feasts, dinner parties, and luncheons to robust buffets for a houseful of guests, Mark has always risen to the occasion. We have worked on menus together, tried out recipes before an event, experimented with soufflés for an entire day in the kitchen, shopped the farmer's market, and laughed all along the way. Mark has seen my family grow up and knows all of their idiosyncrasies along with the allergies of my friends. That's as much information as anyone needs! #LOL

Brandi Anderson has assisted Mark for many of our events and certainly for our Family Weeks in East Hampton for as long as I can remember. Brandi is Mark's right hand on all of these occasions, and even when things might get a little frantic just before serving, Brandi is always smiling.

Peggy and Zezé know me well enough by now that when I use certain words, describe a color, or reference a painting, they know how to interpret it all in a bouquet of flowers. Loose and natural, flowing and trailing, robust and gutsy, or translucent and ethereal, they know the flowers to interpret those words. It is a gift to have a relationship like this. I cherish that . . . and them, of course.

Helena Lehane has a specialized floral design business. As a private contractor, Helena made the retail store that I used to own always look beautiful. Helena is known for using a single type of flower in her bouquets, and there have been many times we have had fun with hundreds of Vanda orchids, parrot tulips, dahlias, and tuberose. No one can get more stems in a vase than Helena.

Annie at Sag Harbor Florist is my go-to for all things floral in East Hampton. Annie has her own farm where many of her flowers are grown. On Thursdays in the summer I get an email from Annie with news of her bounty for the weekend. When I arrive on Friday, my flowers are waiting in buckets in my flower room. My flower therapy begins when I start to arrange, listen to music, and fix a glass of wine.

I also thank my staff that understands my absences, my deadlines, and the otherwise state of panic they see me in.

And my friends, who had patience when I said I was working on the book and therefore could not do something or had to postpone something else, and who just listened when I needed an ear. I am grateful to you all.

And to Barry, there's so much to say, but to summarize, "You are a saint . . . and I am the luckiest girl." And, as you know so well, this is not my last!

Resources

CHINA

Alberto Pinto
Artedona.com/en/Brands/Alberto-Pinto/

Au Bain Marie
aubainmarie.fr/en/

Bardith
bardith.com

Caroline Faison
carolinefaison.com

Fitz & Floyd
fitzandfloyd.com

Giovanna Amoruso-Manzari
Arts de la Table, Paris
artgam@alicedsl.fr

Hermès
hermes.com

Kim Faison
kimfaisonantiques.com

La Tuile à Loup
latuilealoup.com

March
marchsf.com

Michael Devine Ltd.
michaeldevineltd.com

Mikasa
mikasa.com/dinnerware/fine-china/

OKA London
oka.com

Pickard
pickardchina.com

Queen's Gallery, London
royalcollectionshop.co.uk

Ralph Lauren
ralphlaurenhome.com

Replacements, Ltd.
Resource for replacing out-of-production
china and dinnerware
replacements.com

Richard Ginori
richardginori1735usa.com

Royal Copenhagen
Flora Danica pattern
royalcopenhagen.com

Tiffany & Co.
tiffany.com

Wedgwood
wedgwood.com/collections

William Yeoward
williamyeoward.com

LINENS

Bergdorf Goodman
bergdorfgoodman.com

Busatti
busatti.com/en/

Caspari
casparionline.com

D. Porthault
dporthaultparis.com

De Vous à Moi
Brigitte Vermelin
34, rue Michel-Ange, 75016 Paris

Fabricut
fabricut.com

Galerie Muriel Grateau
murielgrateau.com/gallery/

Henry Handwork
henryhandwork.com

Hudson Grace
hudsongracesf.com

Leontine Linens
leontinelinens.com

Maison Valombreuse
valombreuse.fr/en/homepage/

Matouk
matouk.com

The Monogram Shop
themonogramshops.com

Nancy Stanley Waud Fine Linens
Los Angeles, California
nstanleywaud@earthlink.net

Penn & Fletcher
Custom monogramming and embroidery
pennandfletcher.com

Roller Rabbit
rollerrabbit.com

Sferra
sferra.com

Siècle Paris
siecle-paris.com

Simrane
simrane.com

Spoonflower
spoonflower.com

Sue Fisher King
suefisherking.com

FLATWARE

Bergdorf Goodman
bergdorfgoodman.com

Christofle
christofle.com

DeVine Corporation
Distributor and wholesaler
of premium brands
devinecorp.net

Ercuis
ercuis.com

Lapparra
lapparra-orfevre.com/en/

Le Prince Jardinier
princejardinier.fr/en/

Replacements, Ltd.
Resource for replacing out-of-production
silver and flatware
replacements.com

Tiffany & Co.
tiffany.com

STEMWARE

Baccarat
us.baccarat.com/en/home/

James Friedberg
jamesfriedberg.com

Moleria Locchi
artemest.com/artisans/moleria-locchi

Riedel
riedel.com

Roost
roostco.com

Theresienthal
theresienthal.de

Tiffany & Co.
tiffany.com

Two's Company
twoscompany.com

William Yeoward Crystal
williamyeowardcrystal.com

ACCESSORIES

1stdibs
Online marketplace for top dealers,
shops, and galleries
1stdibs.com

A Mano
Tableware, linens, placemats, lighting,
home accessories
amano.bz

And George
Vases, pillows, furniture, objets
andgeorge.com

The Antique and Artisan Gallery
theantiqueandartisangallery.com

Armorial, Paris
Place cards, stationery
armorial.fr/en/

Benneton Graveur
Place cards
shop.bennetongraveur.com

Buccellati
Fine silver objets, jewelry
us.buccellati.com/en

Caspari
Paper products
caspironline.com

Cassegrain
Engraved place cards
cassegrain.fr

Ceylon et Cie
ceylonetcie.com

Christian Dior
Fashion and home accessories
dior.com

Comer & Co.
Antiques and decorative items
comerandco.com

Creel & Gow
creelandgow.com

Frances Palmer Pottery
francespalmerpottery.com

Guinevere
guinevere.co.uk

Hudson Grace
Linens, gifts, tableware, lighting,
home accessories
hudsongracesf.com

Kinsey Marable & Co.
Out-of-print and early editions of books
on entertaining and social history
privatelibraries.com

Mario Luca Giusti
Acrylic stemware and picnicware
mariolucagiusti.com

Mark and Graham
markandgraham.com

Mecox Gardens
mecox.com

The Met Store
The Metropolitan Museum of Art
store.metmuseum.org

Missiaglia
Silver salt and pepper shakers in
the shapes of artichokes, vegetables,
and fruits
missiaglia1846.com

The Monogram Shop
themonogramshops.com

Monticello Gift Shop
monticelloshop.org

One Kings Lane
onekingslane.com

The Real Real
Luxury consignment
therealreal.com

Red Egg
Bench-made contemporary Asian
furniture and home accessories
redegg.com

Rose Tarlow
Furniture, textiles, rugs, lighting, home
accessories
rosetarlow.com

Serena & Lily
serenaandlily.com

Sue Fisher King
suefisherking.com

Thompson + Hanson
Retail nurseries and lifestyle shops
thompsonhanson.com

Vladimir Kanevsky
Fine porcelain flowers and tableware
thevladimircollection.com

The Vogel Bindery
Leather place card holders
vogelbindery.com

Wayfair
Furniture and housewares
wayfair.com

William-Wayne & Co.
william-wayne.com

FLOWERS

Dutch Flower Line
New York
Wholesale distributors (upstairs, see
Milton for topiaries)
dutchflowerline.com

Flower.fr
Paris
flower.fr

FLOWERBX Limited
London
Single flower arrangements
flowerbx.com

G. Page Wholesale Flowers
New York
gpage.com

Holiday Flowers and Plants
New York
Orchids, ferns, shrubs, indoor and
outdoor trees
holidayflowersnyc.com

Moulié Fleurs
Paris
mouliefleurs.com/english/

Plaza Flowers
New York
plazaflowersnyc.com

Sag Harbor Florist
Sag Harbor, Long Island, NY
sagharborflorist.net

Zezé
New York
zezeflowers.com

The End

Image Credits

All images © 2018 by Charlotte Moss except for the following:

Brittany Ambridge: 1, 4 (middle left, bottom left, bottom center), 7 (top), 14, 15, 76, 77, 79 (middle center, middle right, bottom center), 80, 80–81, 83 (all), 84, 85, 86, 87, 88–89, 90, 91, 118, 119, 136, 137, 142, 143, 148–49, 150 (all), 151 (all), 152, 153 (top, bottom), 154, 156, 157, 202, 203, 228, 229, 231 (top left, middle left, middle right), 234–35, 238–39, 240–41, 242–43, 250–51, 272, 274, 275, 279 (top left, bottom right), 280, 281, back endpapers

BFA Images: 2, 3, 4 (top left), 79 (middle left), 112–13, 113, 114 (top, bottom), 115 (all), 116–17

Pieter Estersohn: front endpapers, 4 (top center), 30, 36, 37, 63, 159 (bottom center), 160–61, 161, 162, 163

Courtesy of Fabricut, Ferrara from the Charlotte Moss Collection: 5 (background)

Jean-Pierre Uys: 7 (bottom), 10 (bottom left), 124, 125 (top, bottom), 126 (all), 127 (top, bottom), 129

Melanie Acevedo: 25, 29

Eric Striffler: 52, 134–35, 135, 232, 233 (top), 269

Roth Williams: 53, 62 (top)

Julie Skarratt Photography: 79 (top center), 120–21, 123

Courtesy of Brunschwig & Fils, Carsten check: 82 (background)

Menus by Rory Kotin of Scribe, Ink calligraphy: 82, 92, 99, 102, 119, 128, 133, 137, 143, 168, 226

Paul Myers-Davis: 108 (top, bottom), 109, 110–11

James Merrell: 144, 145 (top, bottom), 146, 147, 155

Johnny Valiant: 164

Courtesy of D. Porthault: 205 (top center, middle left)

Horst P. Horst/*Vogue* © Condé Nast: 205 (top right), 207, 211, 220

Courtesy of Sotheby's: 205 (bottom right), 212–13

Hillwood Estate, Museum & Gardens Archives: 205 (middle right)

Private Collection Photo © Christie's Images/Bridgeman Images: 205 (bottom left), 220 (background), 221

Henry Clarke/Condé Nast Collection/Getty Images: 205 (top left), 208

Cecil Beaton/Condé Nast Collection/Getty Images: 206

Copyright Norman Parkinson Ltd/Courtesy Norman Parkinson Archive: 209

Fred R. Conrad/*The New York Times*/Redux: 210

Hillwood Estate, Museum & Gardens Archives, Photographed by Alex Jamison: 214, 215 (top right, bottom)

Ed Clark/The LIFE Picture Collection/Getty Images: 216

The Lowenherz Collection of Kennedy Photographs, Peabody Archives, The Johns Hopkins University, Orlando Suero, photographer: 217

Edward Steichen/*Vogue* © Condé Nast: 218

Bettmann/Getty Images: 4 (center), 219

Walter Carone/*Paris Match* Collection/Getty Images: 222

Courtesy of Scalamandré, Zebra: 223 (background)

Slim Aarons/Getty Images: 223

Courtesy PA Images: 224

Beth Scanlon: 226 (menu border), 246, 247

"Audrey at Home" by Luca Dotti & Luigi Spinola (Harper Design) © 2015 Luca Dotti, Photograph © The Audrey Hepburn Family Archive: 227

First published in the United States of America in 2018 by
Rizzoli International Publications, Inc.
300 Park Avenue South
New York, New York 10010
www.rizzoliusa.com

ISBN: 978-0-8478-6185-9
Library of Congress Control Number: 2017951933

Recipes on page 225 are from the following sources:
Pêches au vin blanc and Poulet à l'estragon from Elizabeth David's *French Provincial Cooking* (London: Michael Joseph, 1960)
Zuppa di fagioli alla toscana from Elizabeth David's *Italian Food* (London: Macdonald,1954)
Elizabeth David's books are still in print and available via Penguin Books.

For Rizzoli International Publications:
Philip Reeser, Editor
Alyn Evans, Production Manager
Megan Conway, Copy Editor

Design: Dina Dell'Arciprete
Printed and bound in China
2018 2019 2020 2021 / 10 9 8 7 6 5 4 3 2 1